CHARACTER SONGS
FROM
MUSICAL THEATRE

WOMEN'S EDITION

31 SONGS
FROM FEATURED
CHARACTER ROLES

ISBN 978-1-4950-9951-9

HAL•LEONARD®

7777 W. BLUEMOUND RD. P.O. BOX 13819 MILWAUKEE, WI 53213

Visit Hal Leonard Online at
www.halleonard.com

CONTENTS BY SONG

CONTENTS BY SHOW

ADELAIDE'S LAMENT

from *Guys and Dolls*

By Frank Loesser

Slowly

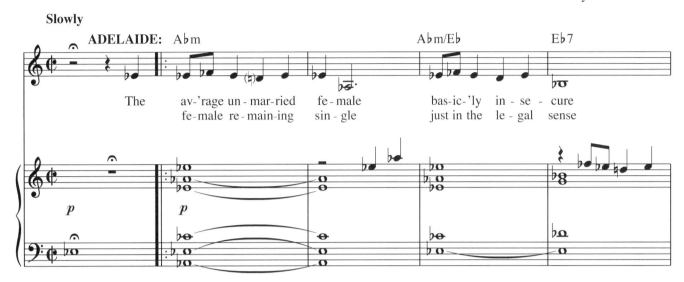

ADELAIDE:

The av-'rage un-mar-ried fe-male bas-ic-'ly in-se-cure
fe-male re-main-ing sin-gle just in the le-gal sense

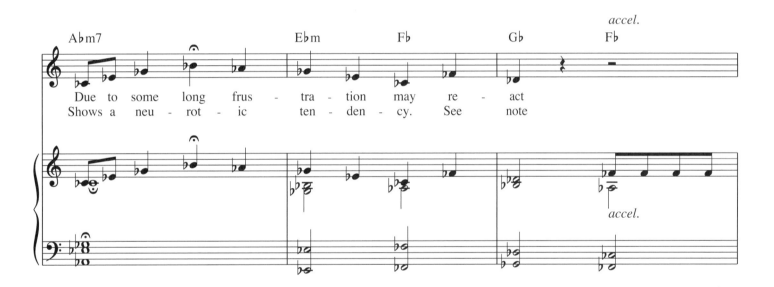

Due to some long frus-tra-tion may re-act
Shows a neu-rot-ic ten-den-cy. See note

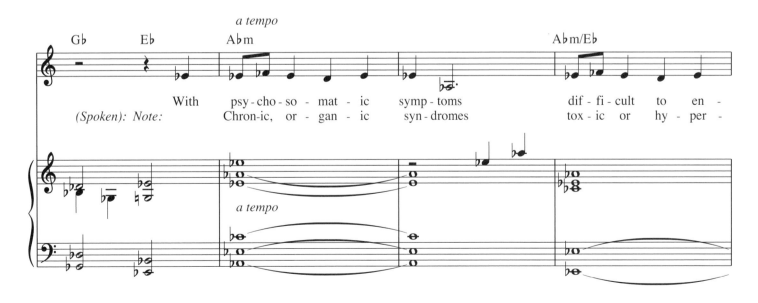

With psy-cho-so-mat-ic symp-toms dif-fi-cult to en-
(Spoken): Note: Chron-ic, or-gan-ic syn-dromes tox-ic or hy-per-

ALTO'S LAMENT

Lyrics by Marcy Heisler
Music by Zina Goldrich

"The Sound of Music"

Pullback

BEGGAR WOMAN'S LULLABY
(Final Sequence)
from *Sweeney Todd*

Words and Music by
Stephen Sondheim

This song was added for the London production of *Sweeney Todd*.

And why should you weep then, my Jo, my jing? Ooh... Your

father's at tea with the Swed - ish king. He'll

bring you the moon on a sil - ver string. Ooh... Ooh...

Quick - ly to sleep then, my Jo, my jing. He'll

GETTING MARRIED TODAY

from *Company*

Music and Lyrics by
Stephen Sondheim

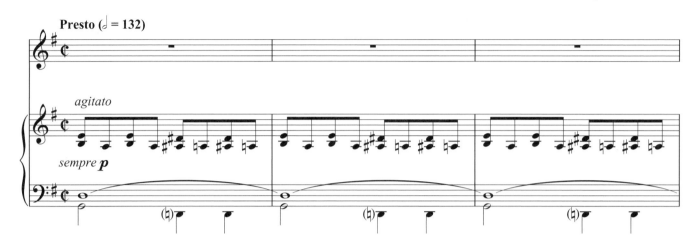

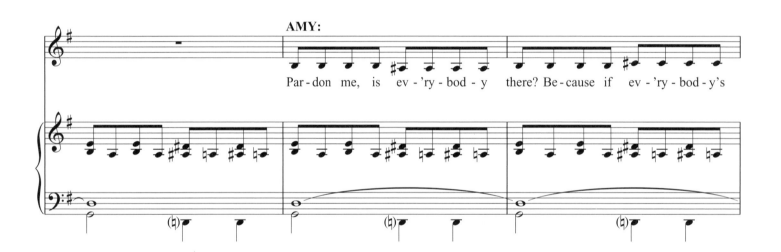

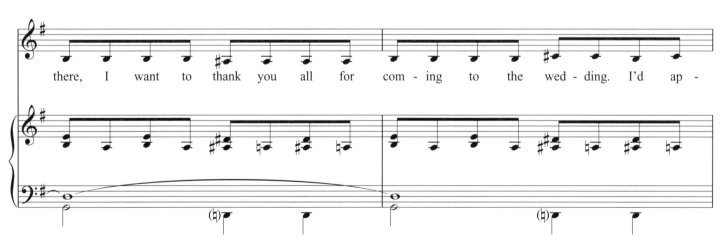

This ensemble has been adapted as a solo for this edition with the composer's blessing.

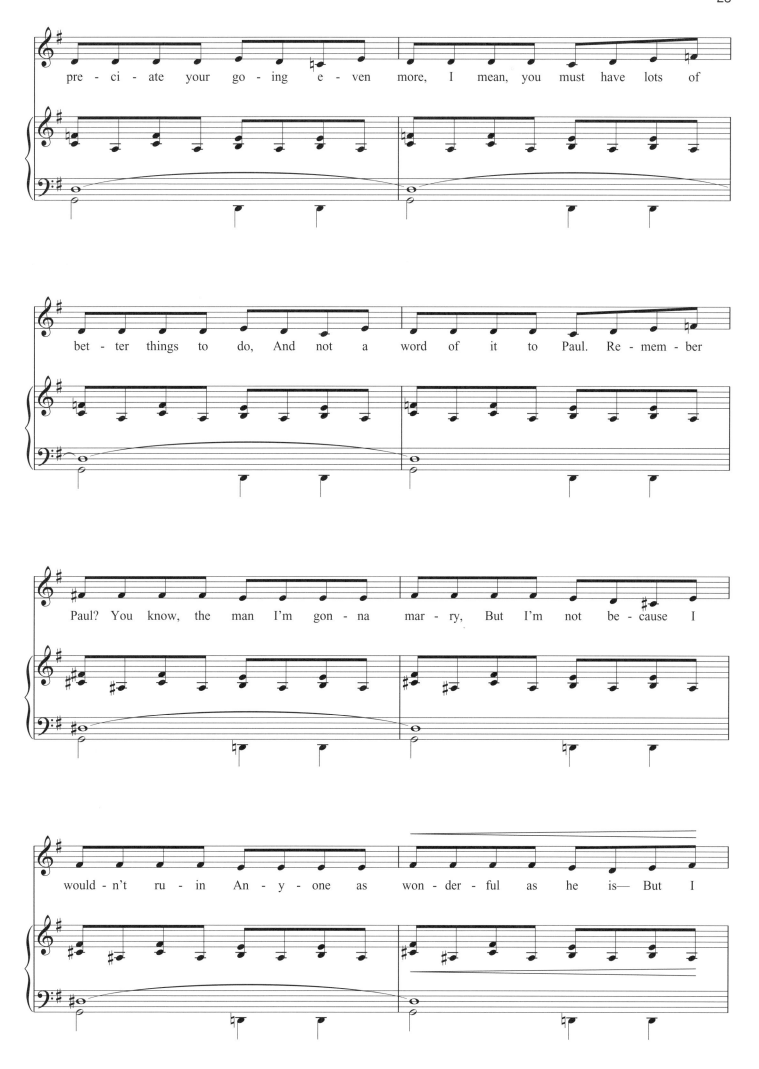

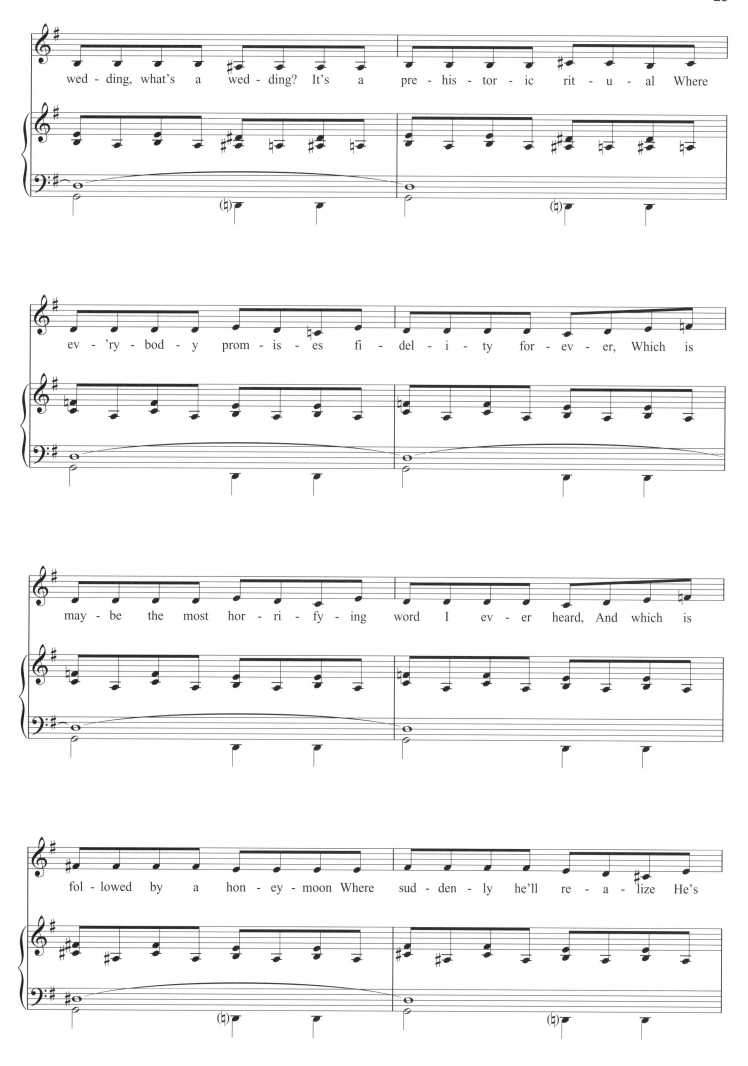

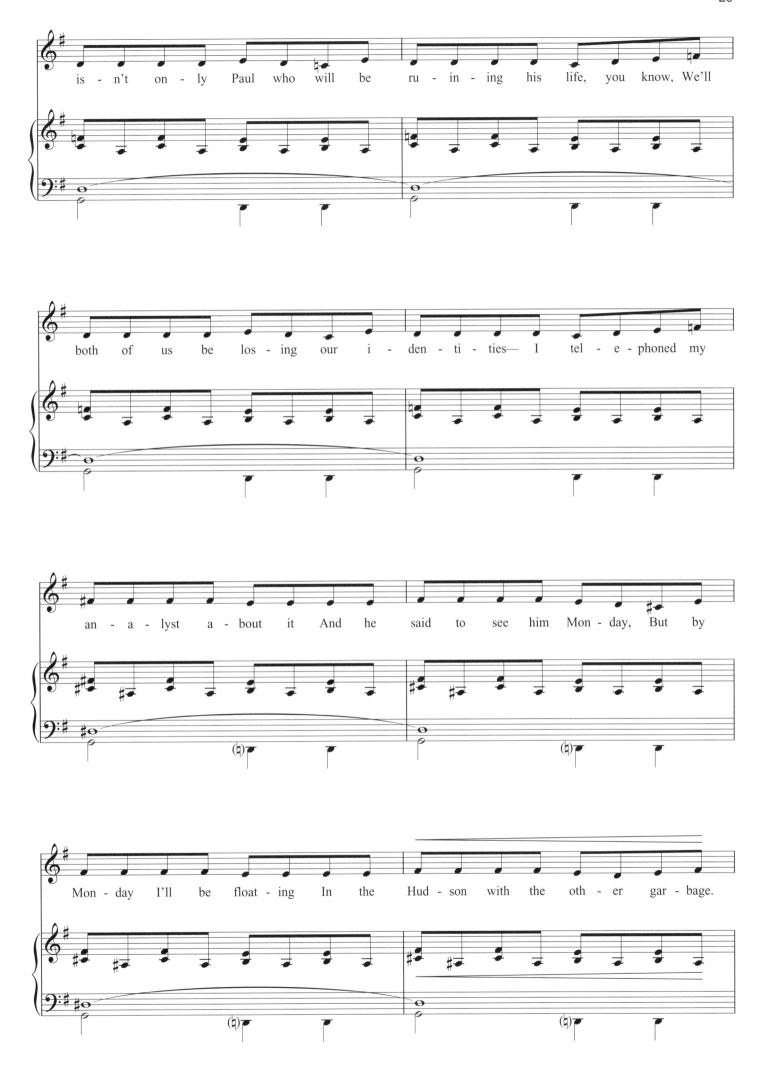

GOOCH'S SONG

from *Mame*

Music and Lyrics by
Jerry Herman

Freely
AGNES:
In 2

(spoken:)

(Sing)

With my wings res-o-lute-ly spread, Mis-sis Burn-side, And my old in-hi-bi-tions shed, Mis-sis Burn-side, I did each lit-tle thing you said, Mis-sis Burn-side.

In 4
Very slowly

I lived! I lived! I lived! I

accel.

Moderately slow 2

al - tered the drape of a drop of my bod-ice And
soft - ened the shape of my brow. _____ I
fol - lowed di - rec - tions, And made some con - nec - tions, But
what do I do now? _____ Who'd

think this Miss Prim would Have o - pened a win - dow As

far as her whim would al - low?_____ And

who would sup - pose it Was so hard to close it, Oh,

what do I do now?_____ I

pol - ished and pow-dered and puffed my - self.____ If

life is a ban-quet I stuffed my - self.____ I

had my mis-giv-ings, But went on a field trip To

find out what liv-ing's a - bout._____ My

thanks for the train-ing Now I'm not com-plain-ing, But

you left some-thing out! In-stead of

Freely

wan-d'ring on with my lone re-morse, I have come back home to com-plete the course. Oh,

Tempo I°

What do I do ---

Spoken:
Mrs. Burnside,

(sung)

I trav-eled to hell in my new ven - eer,____ And look what I got as a sou - ven-ir!____ But still I'll de-fend you as guide and in-struct-or. Would I rec - om-mend you? And how! ____ Al - though I was leer - y, i

thrived on your theo-ry That life can be a wow! ____

Freely

You said there's noth-ing wrong with a harm-less smooch, So I'm gon-na call him

Tempo I°

Burn-side Gooch! Oh, what do I do

now? ____

ff

sfz

HEADS OR TAILS
from *Cowgirls*

Written by Mary Murfitt

I CAIN'T SAY NO
from *Oklahoma!*

Lyrics by Oscar Hammerstein II
Music by Richard Rodgers

It ain't so much a ques - tion of not

know - ing whut to do.   I knowed whut's right and

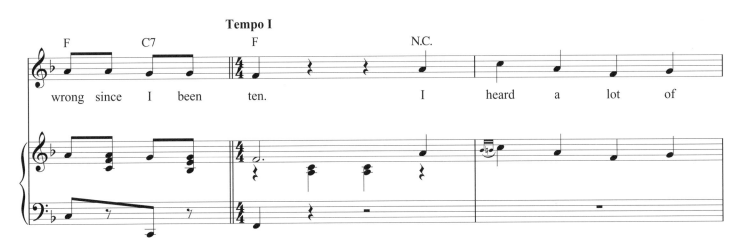

wrong since I been ten.   I heard a lot of

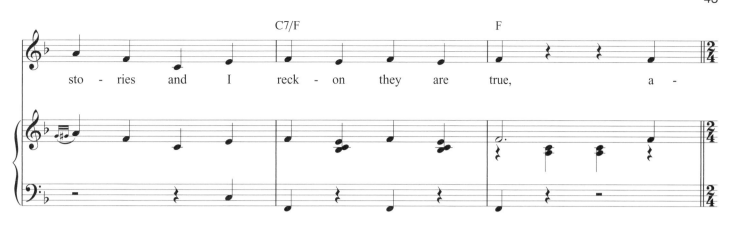

sto - ries and I reck - on they are true, a -

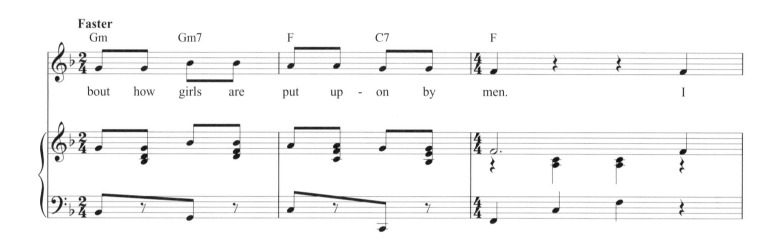

Faster

bout how girls are put up - on by men. I

know I must-n't fall in - to the pit. _____ But when I'm with a fel - ler, I fer -

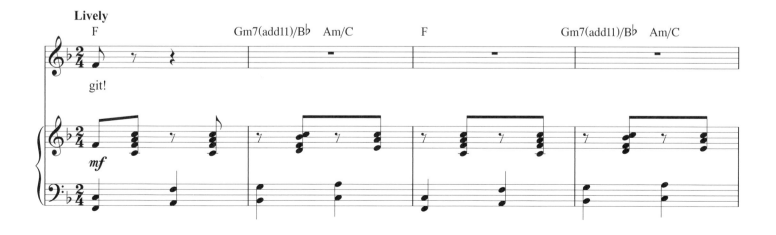

Lively

git!

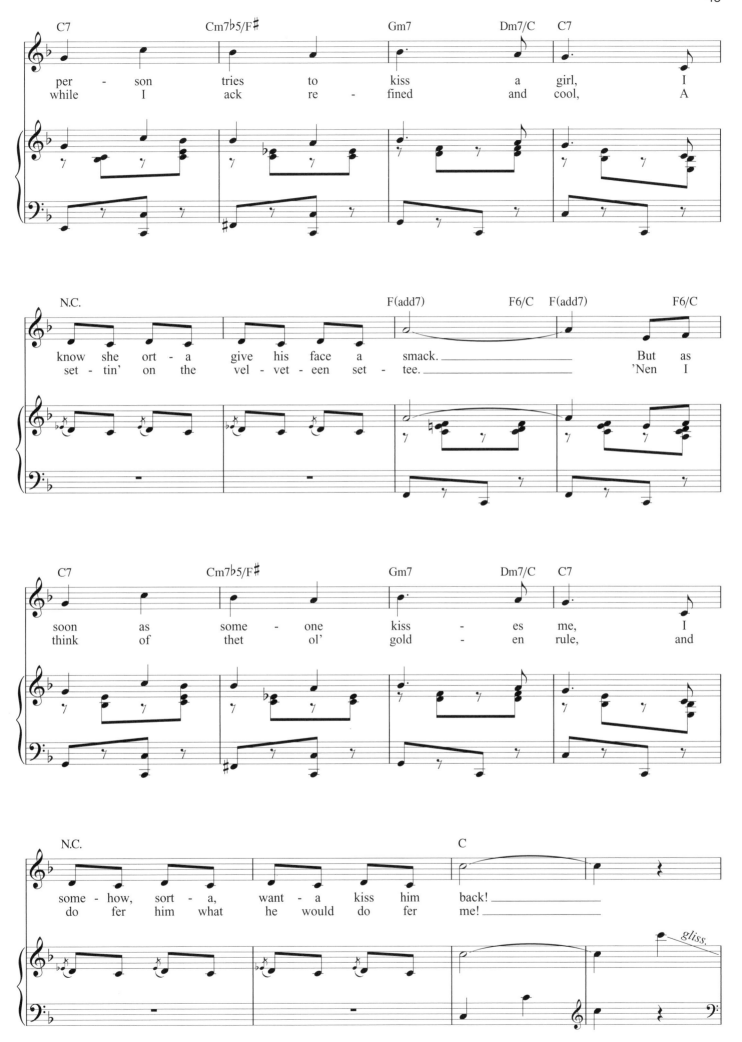

I WANT TO GO TO HOLLYWOOD

from the Broadway Musical *Grand Hotel*

Words and Music by
Maury Yeston

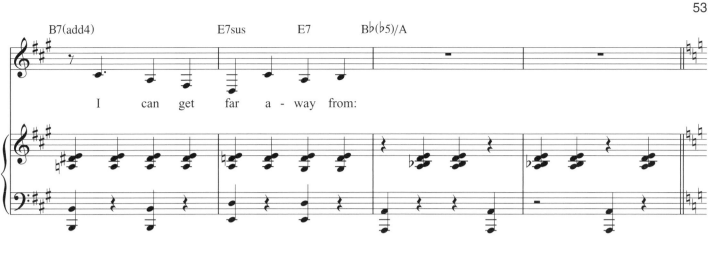

I can get far a - way from:

Fried - rich - stras - se. My cold wa - ter flat. The so - fa

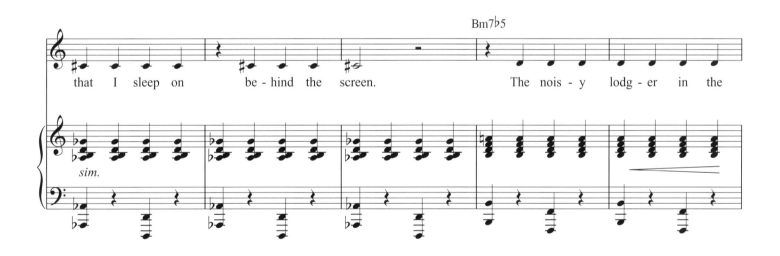

that I sleep on be - hind the screen. The nois - y lodg - er in the

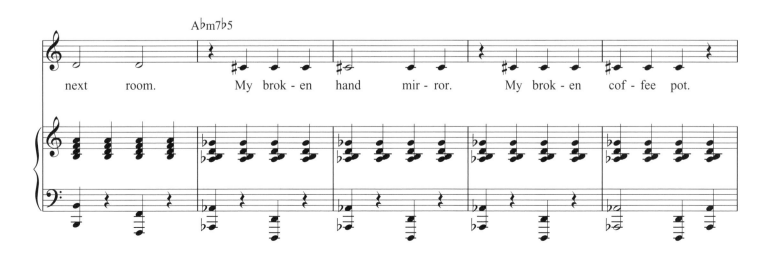

next room. My brok - en hand mir - ror. My brok - en cof - fee pot.

I JUST WANT TO BE A STAR

from *Nunsense*

Words and Music by
Dan Goggin

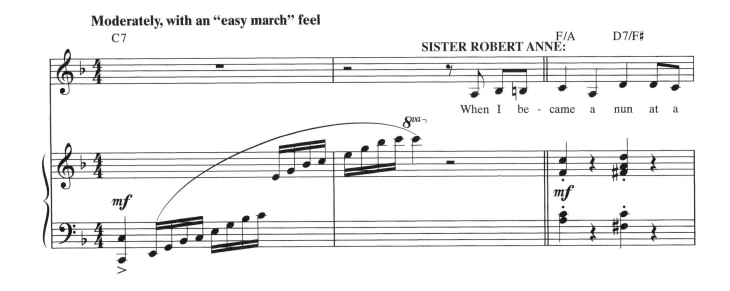

Easy 4

I don't care if I'm ev-er rich or fa-mous. I just want to be a

star. I don't care if you know what my name is,

I just want to be a star. I want to be the

nun who makes you cheer, the nun who's out in front in-stead of at the rear. For

I RESOLVE
from *She Loves Me*

Words by Sheldon Harnick
Music by Jerry Bock

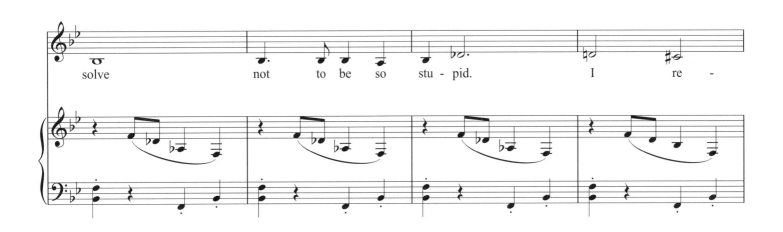

sit - ting duck for Cu - pid. _____ How of - ten I've let him

shoot me down in flames. I re -

solve not to be so trust - ing. It's high

time time that I a - woke. What - ev - er I've got up

here is up here rust - ing. _____ My fem - i - nine in - tu -

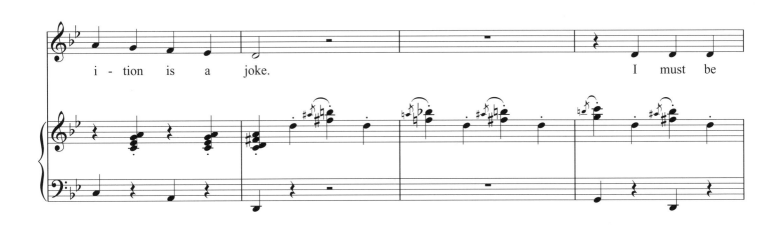

i - tion is a joke. I must be

cou - sin to a cat. I al - ways

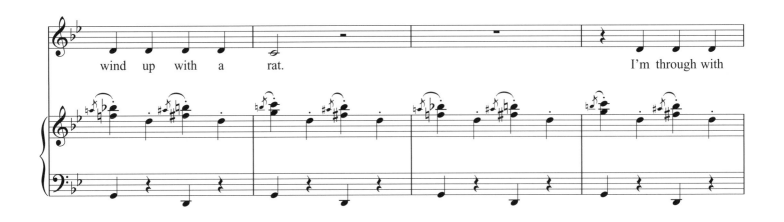

wind up with a rat. I'm through with

mo - men - ta - ry thrills. I find I

can't af - ford the bills. I re -

solve come what may I will

not be this girl one more day.

got to know how come. I re-

solve not to blame the oth - ers, just be -

cause I'm an eas - y mark. I want to know why I

nev - er meet their moth - ers. Where men are con - cerned I'm

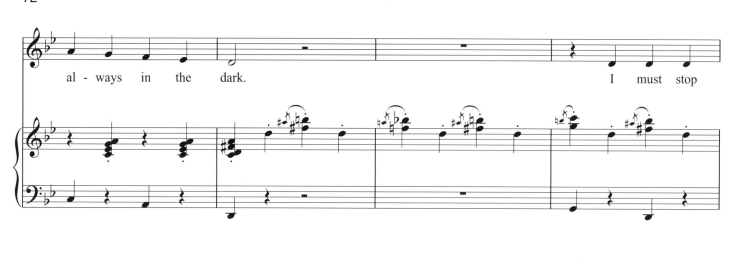

al - ways in the dark. I must stop

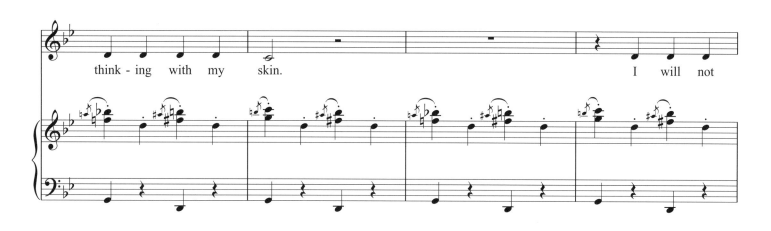

think - ing with my skin. I will not

be a man - do - lin. That some - one

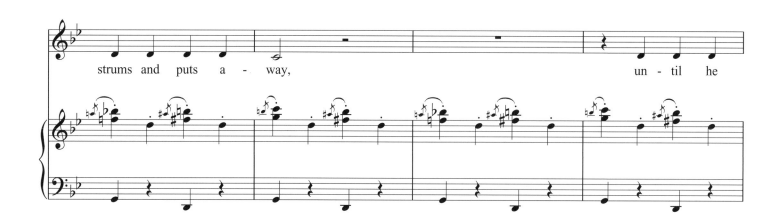

strums and puts a - way, un - til he

gets the urge to play._____ I re-

solve here and now I will

be a dif-ferent girl_____

___ some-how!_____

I WANT TO BE BAD

from *Good News*

Words and Music by
B.G. DeSylva, Lew Brown
and Ray Henderson

Good or bad which is the best for me?

When you're af - ter fun and laugh - ter This ag - gra - vates____ you

Some re - form - er says a warm - er cli - mate a - waits____ you.

Refrain

If it's naught - y to rouge your lips __ Shake your shoul - ders and twist your hips __

What can you do if your load-ed with plent-y Of

hell - th ___ and vig-or? When you're learn-ing what lips are for ___

If it's naught-y to ask for more ___ Let a la-dy con-fess I want _ to be

1. bad.

2. bad. _____

A LITTLE BRAINS, A LITTLE TALENT

from *Damn Yankees*

Words and Music by Richard Adler
and Jerry Ross

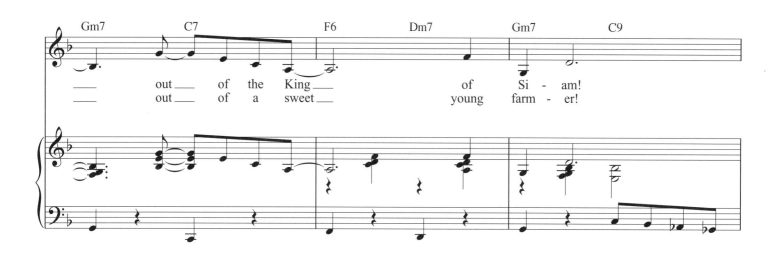

Prince of Wales. It's no great art, __ get - tin' the heart __ of a
pierced his ar - mor. And, I'll bet, __ I can up - set __ ev - 'ry

man _____ on a sil - ver plat - ter.
male _____ in a Yale re - gat - ta!

A lit - tle brains, a

lit - tle tal - ent, with an em - pha - sis on the lat - ter!

You got - ta know just what to say and how to say it.

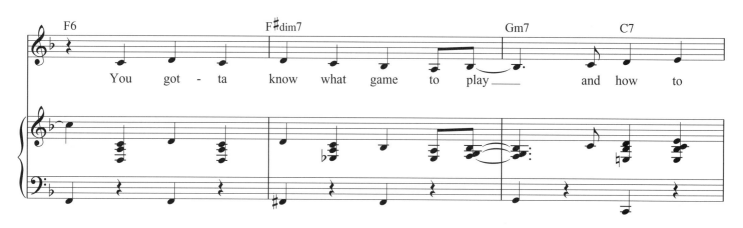

You got - ta know what game to play _____ and how to

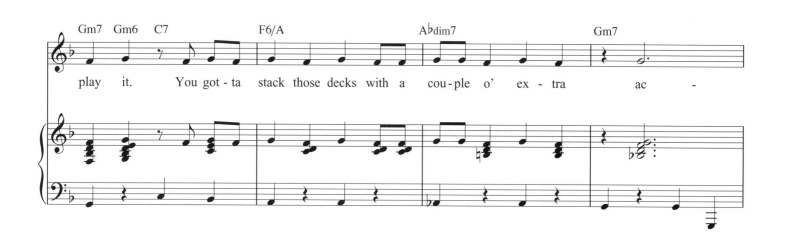

play it. You got - ta stack those decks with a cou - ple o' ex - tra ac -

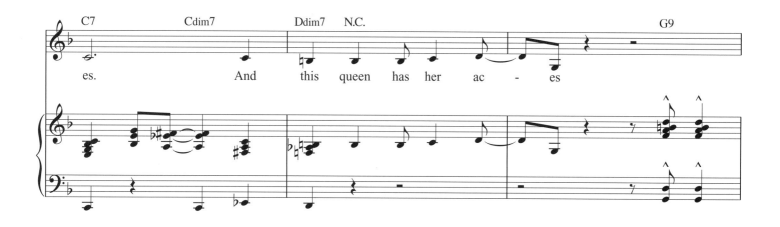

es. And this queen has her ac - es

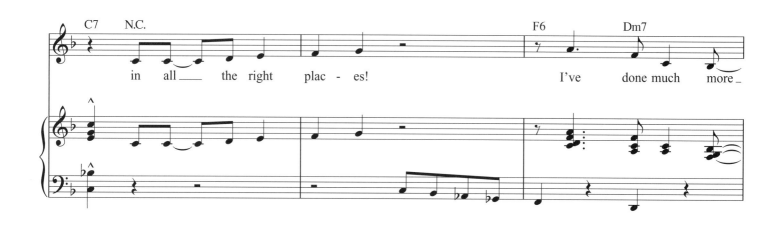

in all ___ the right plac - es! I've done much more _

a lit - tle brains, with an em - pha - sis on the form - er!

Split up a home _ way _ up in Nome _

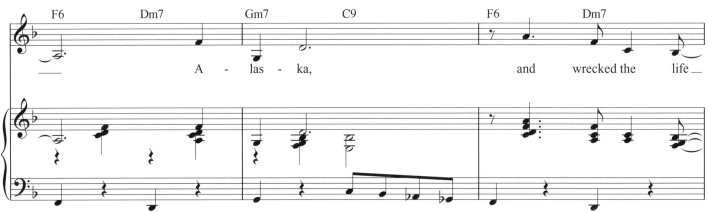

_ A - las - ka, and wrecked the life _

of ___ ev - 'ry wife _____ down in Mad - a - gas - car.

Ask me why ___ weak men - 'll die ___ for me, strong men sim - ply

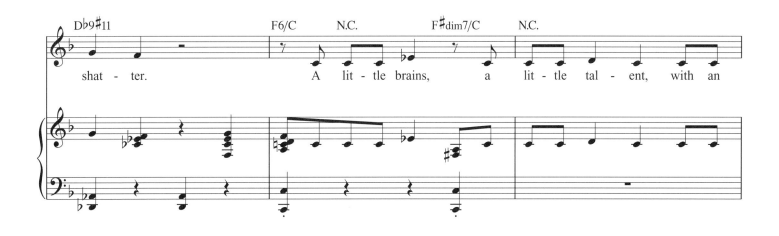

shat - ter. A lit - tle brains, a lit - tle tal - ent, with an

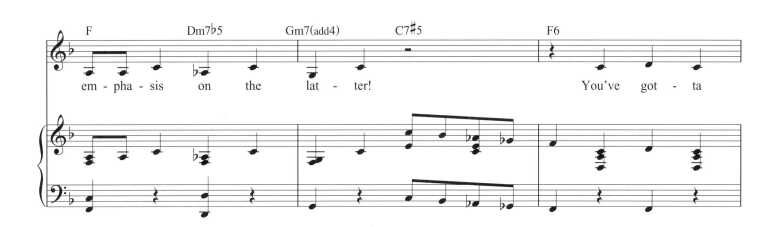

em - pha - sis on the lat - ter! You've got - ta

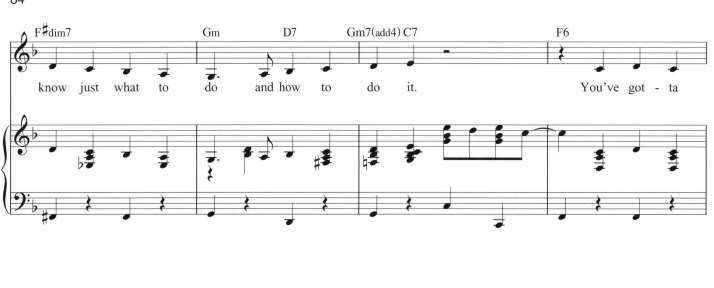

know just what to do and how to do it. You've got-ta

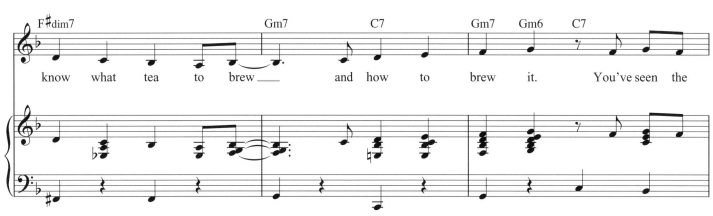

know what tea to brew ____ and how to brew it. You've seen the

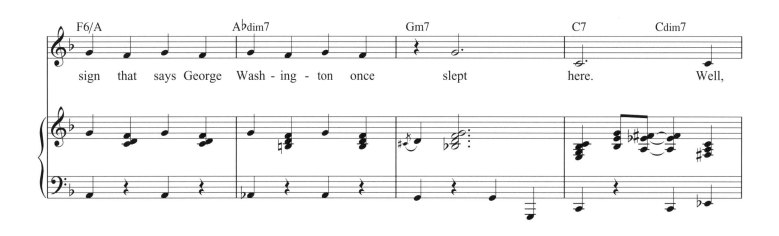

sign that says George Wash - ing - ton once slept here. Well,

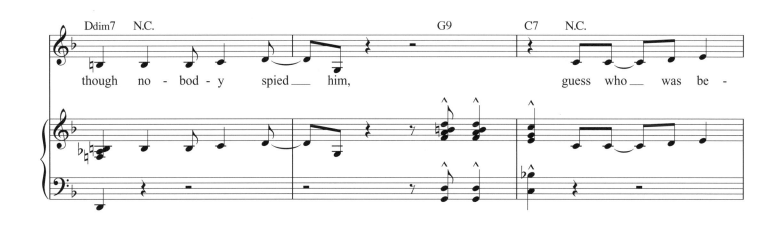

though no - bod - y spied ____ him, guess who ____ was be -

side him? Bring on that boy.__ He'll__ be a toy__

__ for Lo - la. Just one more case__

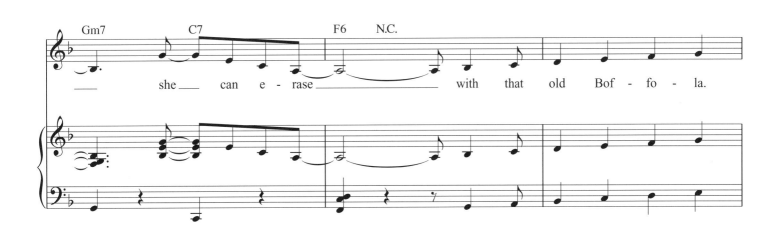

__ she__ can e - rase_____ with that old Bof - fo - la.

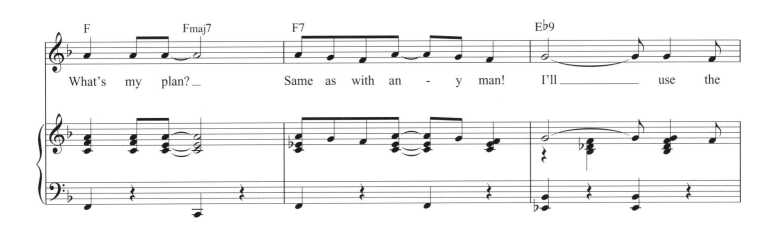

What's my plan?__ Same as with an - y man! I'll_____ use the

IRELAND
from *Legally Blonde*

Music and Lyrics by Laurence O'Keefe
and Nell Benjamin

PAULETTE: *Elle, do you know the number one
reason behind all bad hair decisions?*

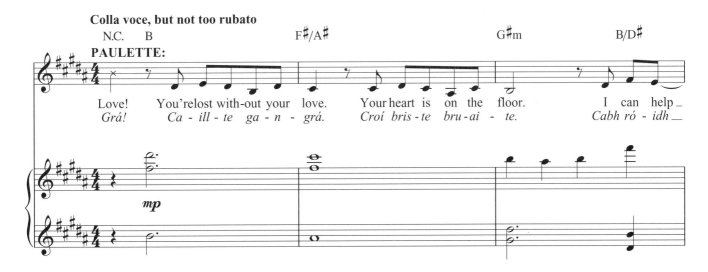

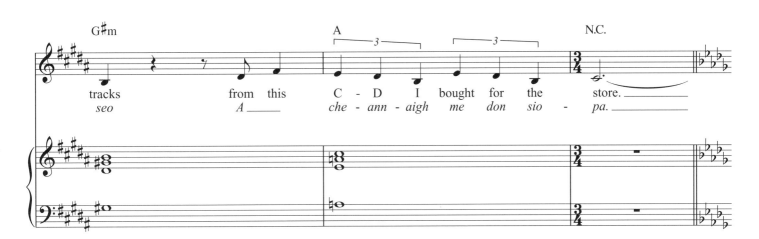

New Age-y Celtic, non rubato

PAULETTE: *Isn't that relaxing? It's called "Celtic Moods."*

When I'm lone - ly or feel - ing de - ject - ed,
Tráth a bhraith - im ua - ig - neach aon - ar - ach,

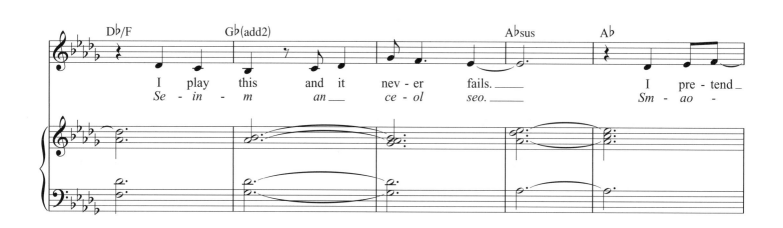

I play this and it nev - er fails.____ I pre - tend___
Se - in - m an___ ce - ol seo.____ Sm - ao -

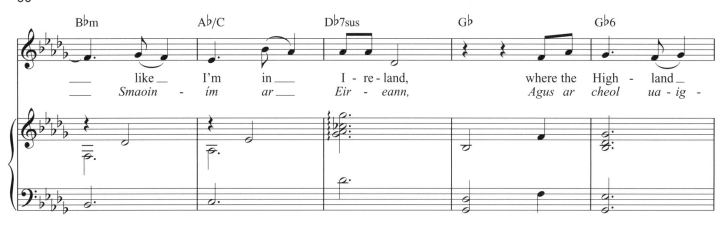

like ___ I'm in ___ I - re - land, where the High - land ___
Smaoin - ím ar ___ Eir - eann, Agus ar cheol ua - ig -

A little faster

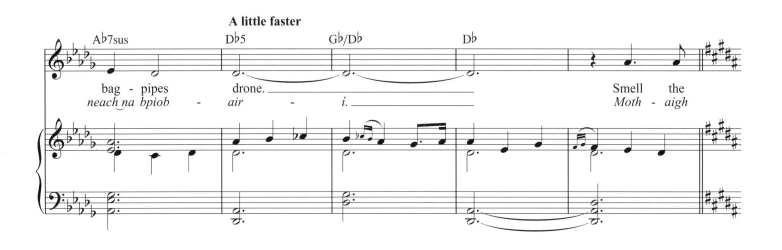

bag - pipes drone. ___ Smell the
neach na bpiob - air - í. ___ Moth - aigh

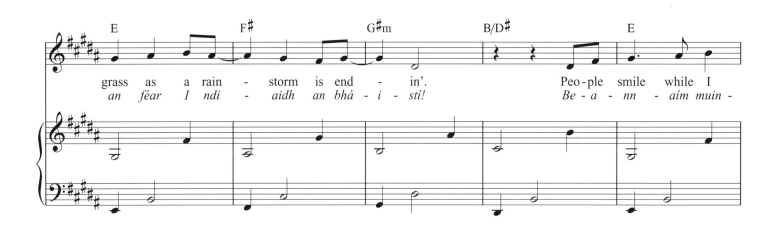

grass as a rain - storm is end - in'. Peo - ple smile while I
an féar I ndi - aidh an bhá - i - stí! Be - a - nn - aím muin -

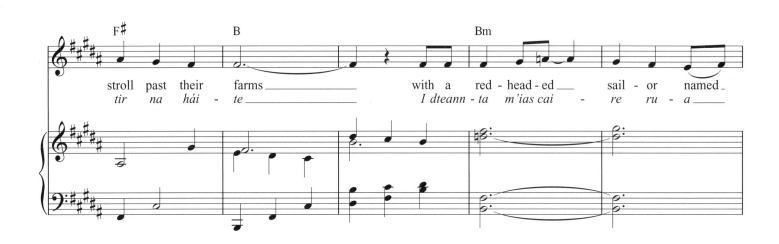

stroll past their farms ___ with a red - head - ed ___ sail - or named
tir na hái - te ___ I dteann - ta m'ias cai - re ru - a ___

92

THE LIFE I NEVER LED
from the Stage Production *Sister Act*

Words by Glenn Slater
Music by Alan Menken

Starts in easy one, steady tempo

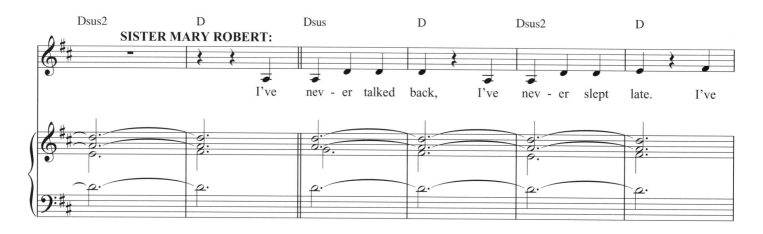

SISTER MARY ROBERT:

I've nev-er talked back, I've nev-er slept late. I've

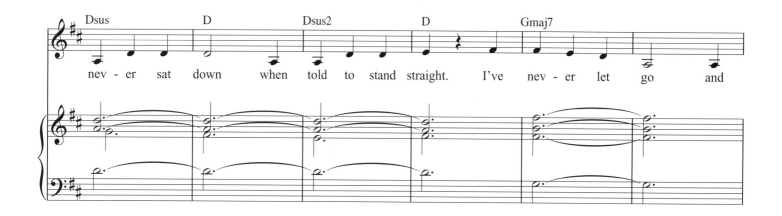

nev-er sat down when told to stand straight. I've nev-er let go and

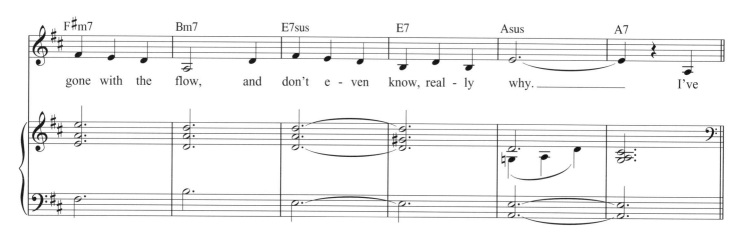

gone with the flow, and don't e-ven know, real-ly why. _____ I've

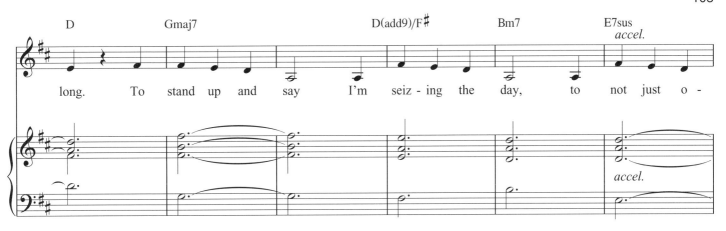

long. To stand up and say I'm seiz-ing the day, to not just o-

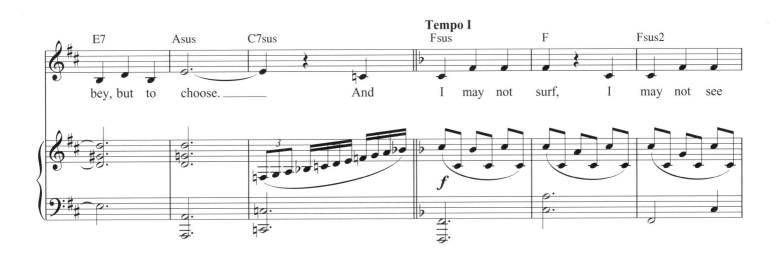

Tempo I

bey, but to choose. _____ And I may not surf, I may not see

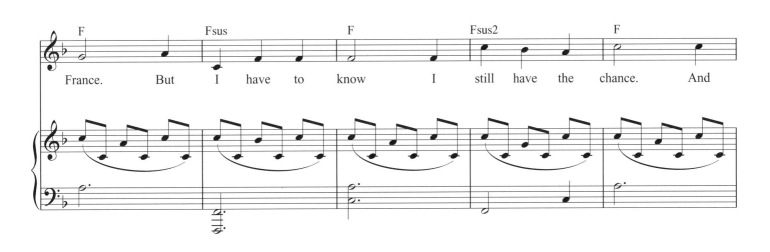

France. But I have to know I still have the chance. And

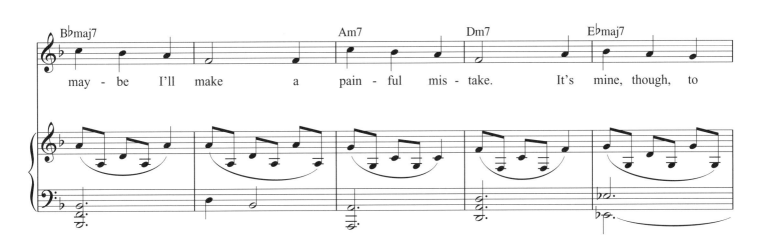

may-be I'll make a pain-ful mis-take. It's mine, though, to

LITTLE GIRLS
from the Musical Production *Annie*

Lyric by Martin Charnin
Music by Charles Strouse

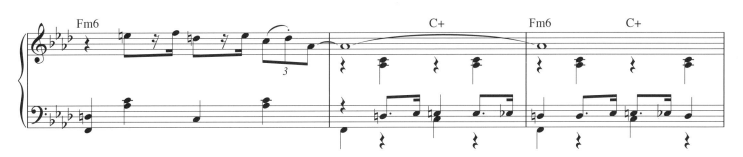

How I hate lit - tle shoes, lit - tle socks and each lit - tle bloom - er. ____

I'd have cracked years a - go if it weren't for my sense of

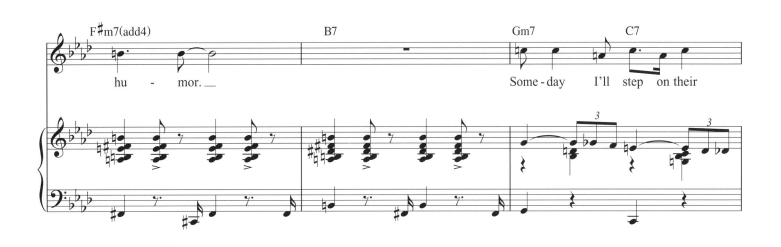

hu - mor. ____ Some - day I'll step on their

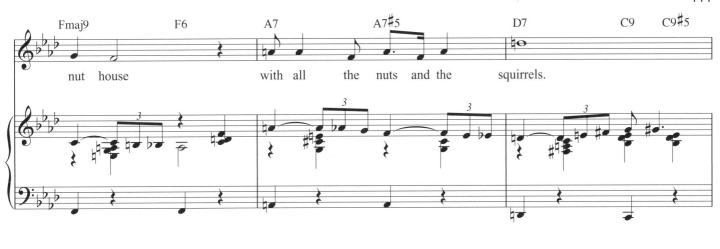

nut house with all the nuts and the squirrels.

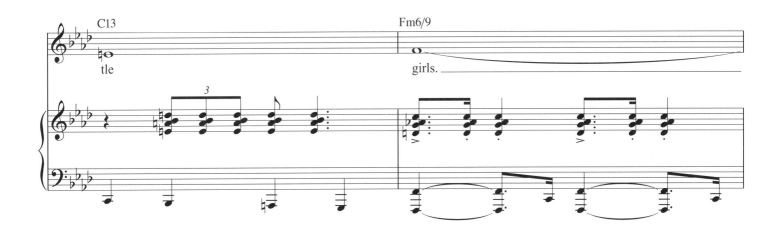

There I'll stay, tucked a-way till the pro - hi - bi - tion of lit -

tle girls.

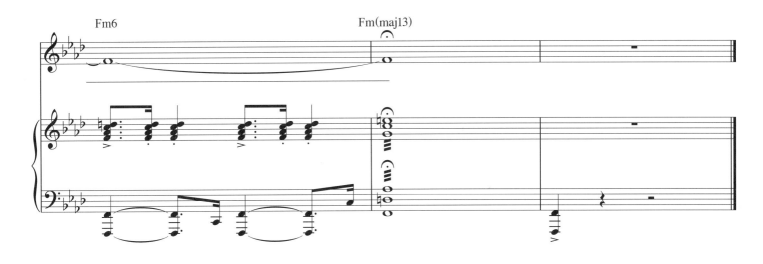

LOOK AT ME, I'M SANDRA DEE

from *Grease*

Lyric and Music by Warren Casey
and Jim Jacobs

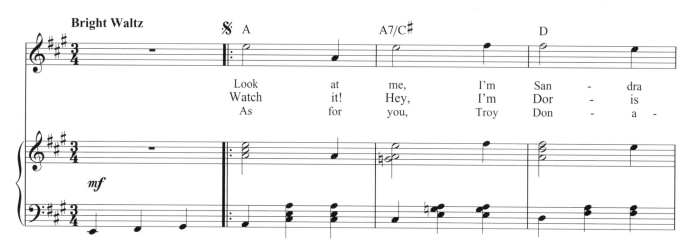

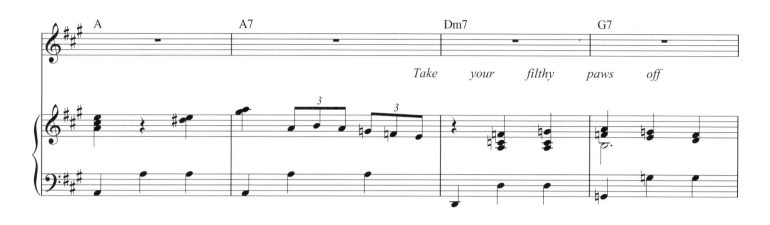

MISS BALTIMORE CRABS

from *Hairspray*

Music by Marc Shaiman
Lyrics by Marc Shaiman
and Scott Wittman

MISS MARMELSTEIN

from *I Can Get It For You Wholesale*

Words and Music by
Harold Rome

124

ONE HUNDRED EASY WAYS TO LOSE A MAN

from *Wonderful Town*

Lyrics by Betty Comden and Adolph Green
Music by Leonard Bernstein

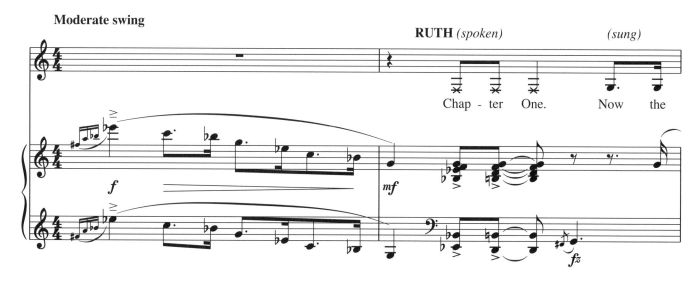

(Spoken flatly)
Just leap out, crawl under the car, say it's the gasket, and fix it in two seconds flat with a bobby pin.

bat your eyes and say, "What _ a ro - man - tic spot we're in." __

That's a good way to lose __ a man. __ He takes you to a base - ball game, you

sit knee to knee. __ He says, "The next man up at bat will bunt, you'll see." ___ Don't

Just say, "Bunt? Are you nuts?! With no outs, two men on base, and a left-handed batter coming up, he'll walk right into a triple play, just like it happened in the fifth game of the World Series in 1923."

say, "Oooh, what's a bunt? This game's too hard for lit - tle me." __

life - guard at the beach that all the girl - ies a dore _____ Swims

rall.

brave - ly out to save you through the o-cean's roar, ___ Don't say, "Oh, thanks, I would have drowned in

Just push his head under
water and yell, "Last one
in is a rotten egg" and race
him back to shore.

a tempo

just one sec-ond more." _ That's a swell way to lose __ a man. _ You've

found your per - fect mate and it's been love from the start. _____ He

rall.

whis - pers, "You're the one to who I give my heart." __ Don't say, "I love you, too, my dear, let's

Just say, "I'm afraid you've made a grammatical
error. It's not "To who I give my heart," it's
"To whom I give my heart." -- You see,
with the use of the preposition "to," "who"
becomes the indirect object, making the use of
"whom" imperative; which I can easily
show you by drawing a simple chart."

a tempo

nev - er, nev - er part." __ That's a fine way to lose __ a man. __ A

Tempo II (Faster)

fine, fine, fine, fine way to lose a man, A dan - dy way _____ to lose a

Slow and free

man. __ Just be more well in - formed than he, You'll nev - er

POOR UNFORTUNATE SOULS

from *The Little Mermaid – A Broadway Musical*

Music by Alan Menken
Lyrics by Howard Ashman

URSULA: *My dear sweet child, it's what I live for.*
To help unfortunate merfolk like yourself.

Tentaclely Teutonic

URSULA: *Poor souls with no one else to turn to.*

URSULA:

I'll ad-mit that in the past I've been a nas-ty. They were-n't

kid-ding when they called me, well, a witch. But you'll find that now-a-days, I've

mend-ed all my ways, re-pent-ed, seen the light and made a switch, true? Yes, And I

for-tu-nate-ly know a lit-tle mag-ic. It's a tal-ent that I al-ways have pos-

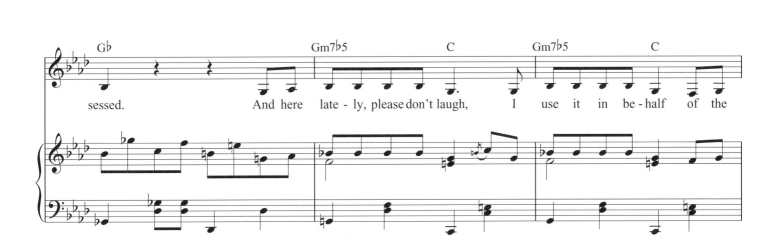

sessed. And here late-ly, please don't laugh, I use it in be-half of the

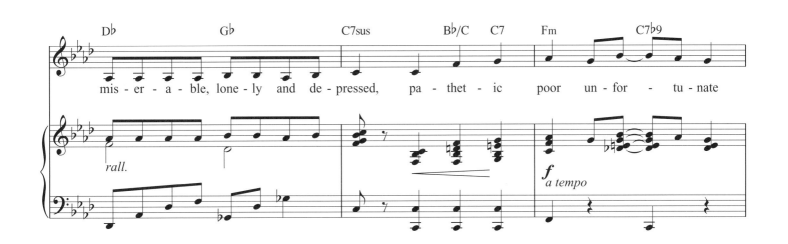

mis-er-a-ble, lone-ly and de-pressed, pa-thet-ic poor un-for-tu-nate

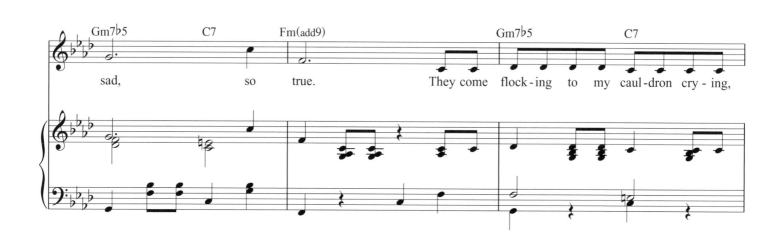

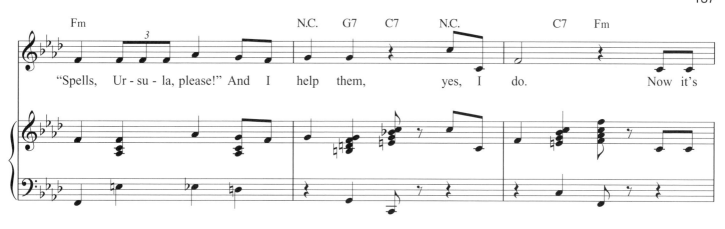

"Spells, Ur-su-la, please!" And I help them, yes, I do. Now it's

Slower, poco rubato

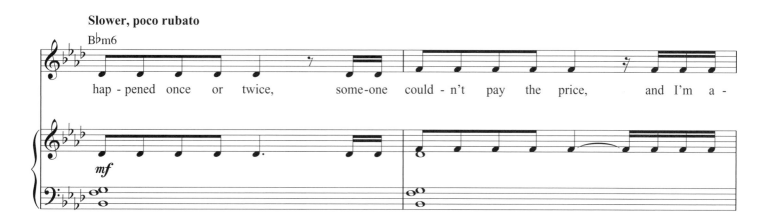

hap-pened once or twice, some-one could-n't pay the price, and I'm a-

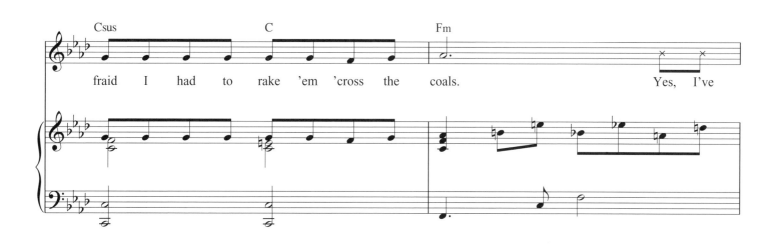

fraid I had to rake 'em 'cross the coals. Yes, I've

had the odd com-plaint. But on the whole I've been a saint to those

SPECIAL
from the Broadway Musical *Avenue Q*

Music and Lyrics by Robert Lopez
and Jeff Marx

*Possible cut to ** for auditions.

your guard. ___ When your date's in the bath-room, I'll

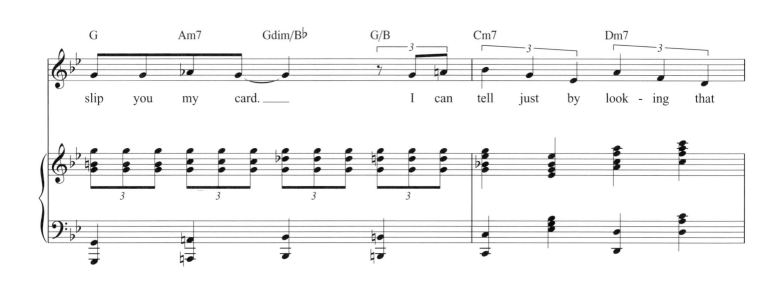

slip you my card. ___ I can tell just by look-ing that

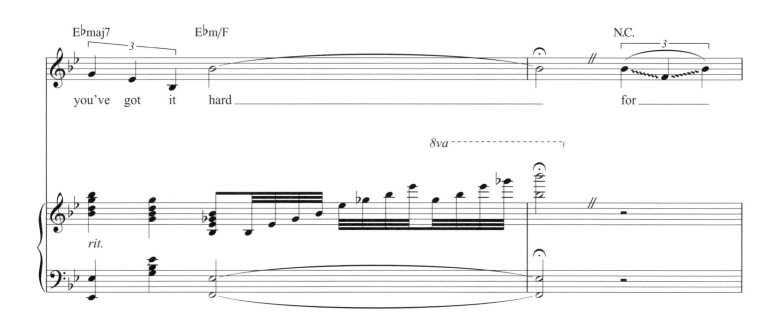

you've got it hard ___ for ___

SOMEWHERE THAT'S GREEN

from *Little Shop of Horrors*

Music by Alan Menken
Lyrics by Howard Ashman

Tempo ad lib

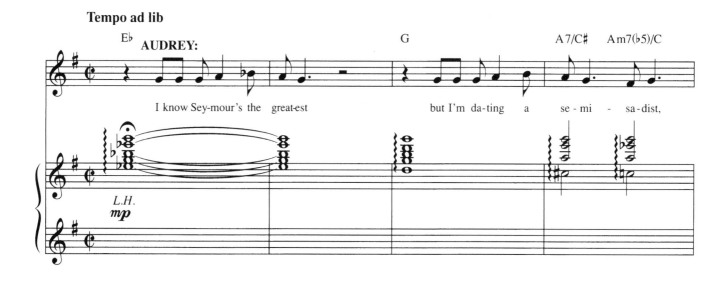

AUDREY:
I know Sey-mour's the great-est but I'm da-ting a se-mi-sa-dist,

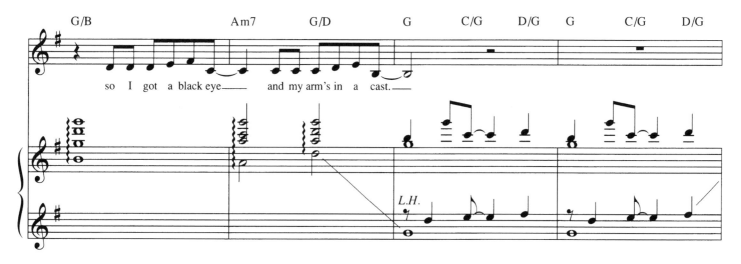

so I got a black eye___ and my arm's in a cast.___

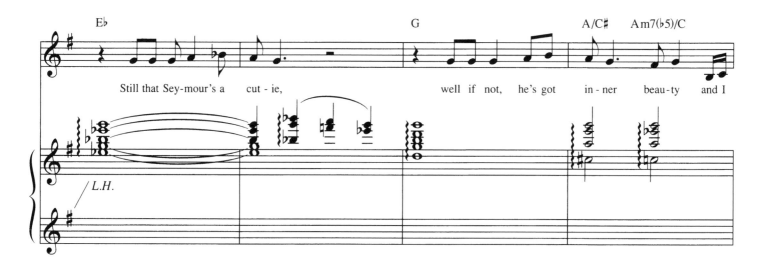

Still that Sey-mour's a cut-ie, well if not, he's got in-ner beau-ty and I

SURABAYA-SANTA

from *Songs for a New World*

Music and Lyrics by
Jason Robert Brown
Additional Material by Kristine Zbornik

Rubato

looked in my eyes and you asked me my name, and I trem-bled be-fore you like a ba-by and

gen - tly I kissed you. *8va‑ ‑ ‑ ‑ ‑ ‑ ‑* (Who could re - sist you?)

a tempo

You took me heart and soul. And be -

gliss.

fore I had a chance to take con - trol, we re - tir - ed to your pal - ace on the

I know by now I'll nev-er claim you___ for my own.

I've been re-signed to spend my Christ-mas-es a-lone, and so "Au'r-

'voir," Nick. It's grand, Nick. I don't pre-tend to un-der-stand, Nick.

I saw you look at Blit-zen long and lov-ing-ly

the way you used to look at me.

I have sat twen-ty years in this draugh-ty re-treat as the lat-est in the line of "Mrs. Claus-es." I've sat here and won-dered what you want from me. But you

I don't sup- pose you'd ev-er want me___ by your side.

I know you now; you want a play-thing, not a bride. So on your

way, Nick. Sha-lom, Nick. Don't feel the need to hur-ry home, Nick!

Should I need com-fort in a cold and___ bit-ter storm,

I've got the elves to keep me warm.

Spoken: *Oh Nick! Nick, I didn't mean it! I'm just going crazy…*

…all cooped up in here.   *Oh, Nick!*

Please take me with you.   *Please, I'm your wife, damn it.*   *Isn't there one ounce of human…*

When you re - turn I will be man - y miles a - way.

I'll have my law - yer call your law - yer New Year's Day. That's all for

me, Nick. Gang - way, Nick. I'll miss you less than I can say, Nick!

Have fun with all the lit - tle boys a - long your route.

I'll get the man-sion and the fac-to-ry to boot.

I will not wait un-til the snow be-neath me thaws.

I will es - cape your San - ta

colla voce

Vivace

Claws!

sffz

TAKE BACK YOUR MINK

from *Guys and Dolls*

By Frank Loesser

Very Slowly

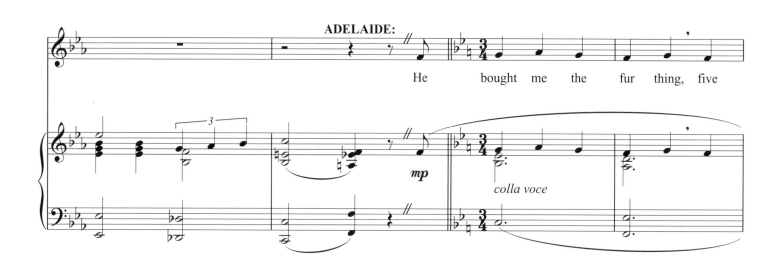

ADELAIDE:

He bought me the fur thing, five

colla voce

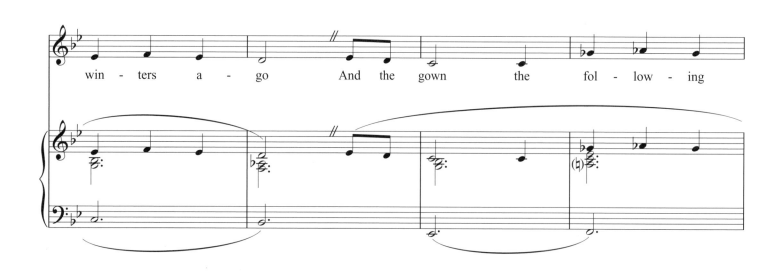

win - ters a - go And the gown the fol - low - ing

Take back the gown, the shoes and the hat

I may be down but I'm not flat as all that

freely

I thought that each ex - pen - sive gift you'd ar - range was a

to - ken of your es - teem. Now when I think of what you

THIS PLACE IS MINE

from *Phantom*

Words and Music by
Maury Yeston

Slowly ♩ = 60

CARLOTTA:

Where does the time____ fly? Sim - ply too few

Faster ♩ = 112

ho - urs in the day! Oh, a di - va's work is nev-

er done, no re - lief, no____ time____ for fun, not____

66

life will start. I'll be

69

out on the stage look-ing great and half my age, ev-'ry

71

chance I get I'll get 'em on their feet. I will

73

burn, I will scheme, I will re-al-ize my dream. 'cause if

THAT'S RICH
from Disney's *Newsies the Musical*

Music by Alan Menken
Lyrics by Jack Feldman

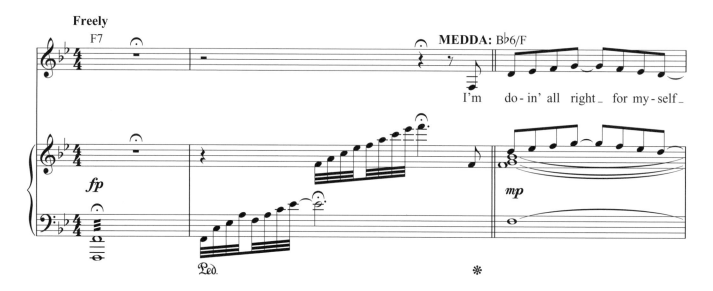

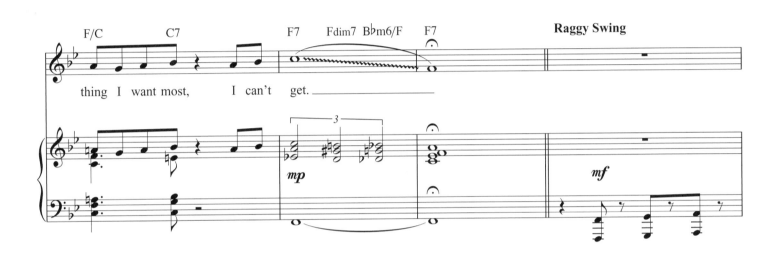

THEY DON'T KNOW

from *Thoroughly Modern Millie*

Music by Jeanine Tesori
Lyrics by Dick Scanlan

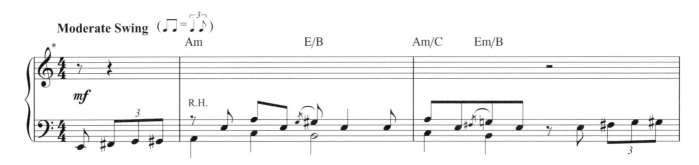

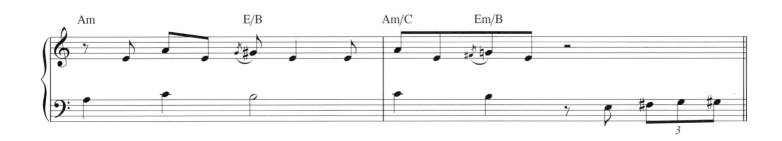

They don't know _ my flair for _ the dra-mat-ic. Not a clue _ the

tal-ent I pos-sess. Pret-ty girls, _ but not much in the at-tic.

*Recorded a half step lower.

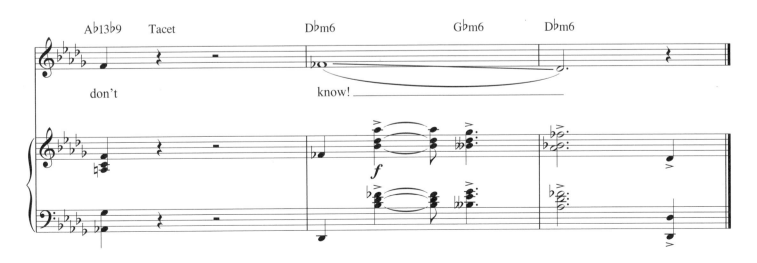

A TRIP TO THE LIBRARY

from *She Loves Me*

Words by Sheldon Harnick
Music by Jerry Bock

MISS RITTER: *(Spoken before the introduction) Let me tell you, you've never seen anything like that library. So many books. . . so much marble. . . so quiet!*

And sud-den-ly all of my con-fi-dence drib-bled a-way with a pit-i-ful plop. My head was be-gin-ning to swim and my fore-head was cov-ered with cold per-spi - ra - tion. I

start-ed to reach for a book and my hand aut-o-mat-i-c'lly came to a stop.   I

don't know how long I stood fro-zen, a vic-tim of pan-ic and mor-ti-fi - ca - tion.____

With Freedom

Oh, _____ how I want-ed to flee _____ when a kind - ly voice, a

rall.   **Moderato**

gen - tle voice whis-pered "Par-don me."

And there _ was this dear, sweet, clear-ly re-spec-ta-ble thick-ly be-spec-ta-cled

man who stood _ by my side and qui-et-ly said _ to me "Ma'am,

Don't mean _ to in-trude, but I was just won-der-ing are you in need _ of some

help?" I said "no . . . Yes, I am!"

mf (*mf*)

The next __ thing I know I'm sip - ping hot choc - 'late and

tell-ing my trou - bles to Paul, whose ten - der brown eyes kept send-ing com-pas - sion-ate

looks. A trip __ to the li - brar - y _____ has made _ a new

girl of _ me, _____ for sud - den-ly I can _ see ____ the mag - ic of

books.

I

have to ad-mit in the back of my mind, I was pray-ing he would-n't get fresh.

And

all of the while I was won-der-ing why an il - lit - er-ate girl should at - tract him.

Then

all of a sud-den he said that I could-n't go wrong with "The Way of All Flesh."

Of

course, it's a nov-el, but I did-n't know or I cer-tain-ly would-n't have smacked him. _____ Well, he gave me a

smile, _____ that I could-n't re - sist, _____ and I knew at once how

rall. **Moderato**

much I liked this op - tom - e - trist.

You know_ what this dear, sweet, slight-ly be - spec - ta-cled gen-tle-man said _ to me

next? He said __ he could solve this prob-lem of mine. __ I said "How?"

He said __ if I'd like he'd will-ing-ly read __ to me some of his fa - vor-ite

things. I said "When?" He said "Now." His nov - el ap-

proach seemed high-ly sus-pi - cious and pos-si-bly dan - ger-ous too. I told __ my-self

reading a - loud as I cook. As long as he's there to read there's quite a good

chance in - deed, a chance that I'll nev - er need to o - pen a

Rubato

book! Un-like some-one else some-one I dim-ly re - call.

a tempo

I know he'll on - ly have eyes for me, my op - tom - e - trist Paul.

WHATEVER LOLA WANTS
(Lola Gets)
from *Damn Yankees*

Words and Music by Richard Adler
and Jerry Ross

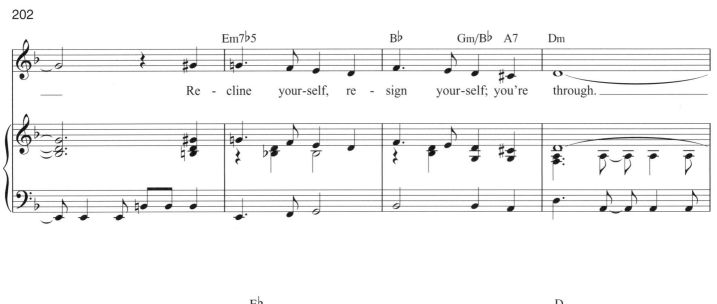

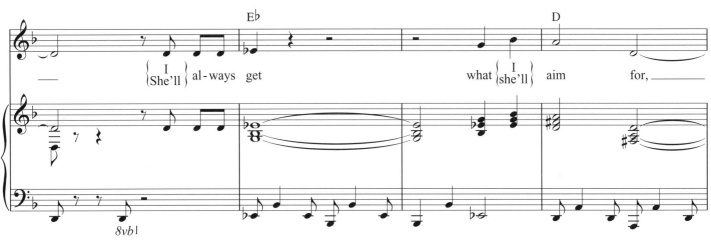

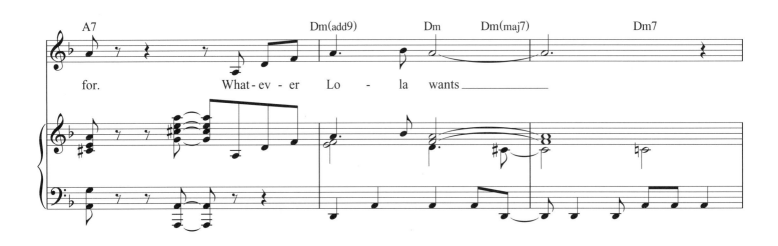

WAITING
from *The Addams Family*

Words and Music by
Andrew Lippa

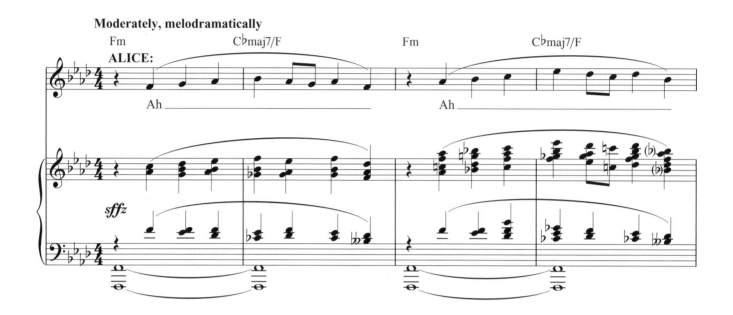

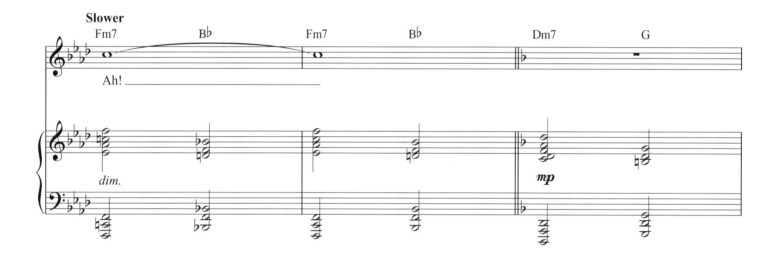

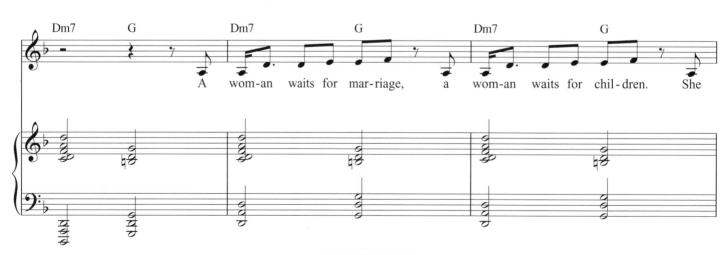

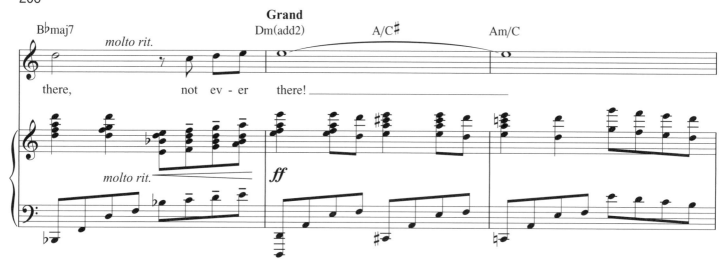

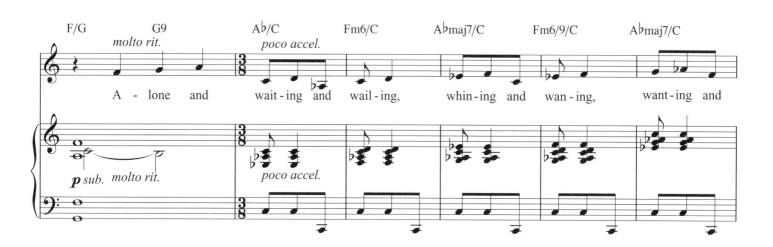

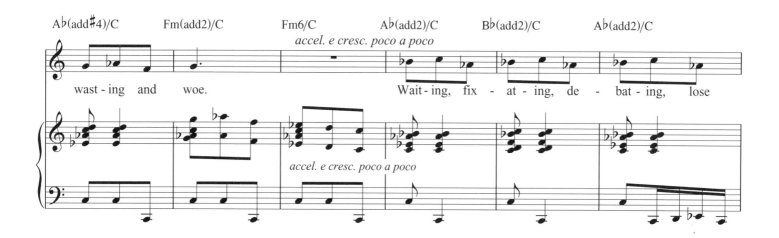

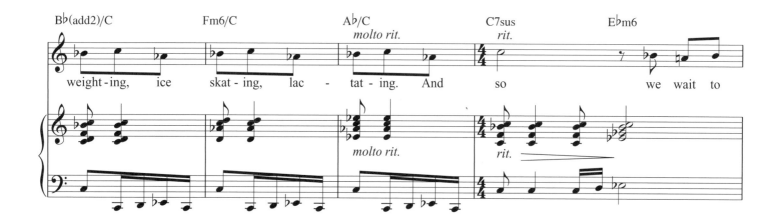

WHEN YOU GOT IT, FLAUNT IT

from *The Producers*

Music and Lyrics by
Mel Brooks

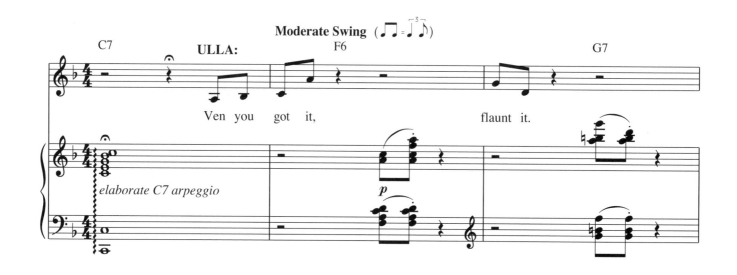

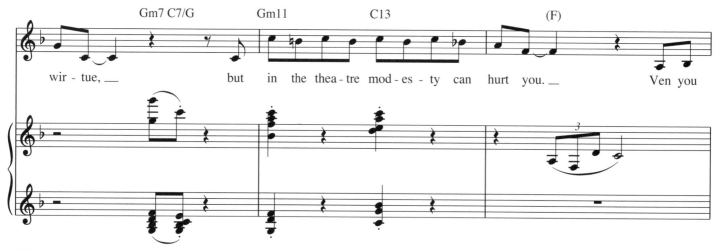

Ulla sings this song with a Swedish accent in the show.